HOW THINGS WORK

WICKED
WHEELS

p

This is a Parragon Publishing Book
This edition published in 2001

Parragon Publishing
Queen Street House
4 Queen Street
Bath BA1 1HE, UK

Copyright © Parragon 2000

ISBN 0-75255-301-1

Printed in Dubai, U.A.E.

Produced by
Monkey Puzzle Media Ltd
Gissing's Farm
Fressingfield
Suffolk IP21 5SH
UK

Designer: Tim Mayer
Cover design: David West Children's Books
Editor: Linda Sonntag
Editorial assistance: Lynda Lines and Jenny Siklós
Indexer: Caroline Hamilton
Project manager: Katie Orchard

CONTENTS

RACING BIKE

No frame tubes
The frame is one piece of molded material called carbon fiber composite. It is extremely light and strong, shaped to withstand all the main stresses put on it without any excess material or weight.

No freewheel
If you stop pedaling on a sprint or racing bike, the pedals keep turning. There is no freewheel, like on a normal bike, that allows the pedals to keep still while the bicycle rolls along.

ON THE ROAD

Speed bicycles are too specialized to ride on roads. The basic design of the road racer, or touring bike, with its down-curved drop-handlebars, has not changed for more than 50 years.

No spokes
As a spoke moves through the air, both turning with the wheel and moving forward with it, this creates air resistance, or friction. The solid, spokeless wheel cuts out the air friction of the 30–40 normal spokes.

No air-filled tires
A cycle track is very flat, without lumps and bumps. So the speed or sprint bike needs only thin, solid rubber treads.

No left stays
The back wheel is fixed to one side of the frame—like the front wheel—for the same reason.

No pedal clips
Expert cyclists pull the pedal up as well as push it down, for greater power and speed. Older style pedals had clips and straps that fitted around a cycling shoe. Newer ones have clips that attach to clips on the soles of the shoes, similar to ski bindings that clip ski boots to skis.

BICYCLE SPEEDS

In a road race, a cyclist needs air-filled tires to iron out bumps in the road, gears to cope with the ups and downs of hills, and brakes to maneuver between competitors or avoid obstacles. But a cycle track is smooth and banked, usually indoors, empty aside from competitors, and exactly the same for every circuit. So the speed or sprint (short race) bicycle is the most stripped-down cycling machine available. Cyclists zoom along at 40mph (60kph) or more in races, with top speeds on specially-modified cycles of over 60mph (100kph).

Elbow rests

The rider rests her or his elbows on these "shelves" while gripping the handlebars above. The streamlined, torpedo-shaped ends keep the elbows from slipping off sideways.

No controls

There are no brakes or gears, so the handlebars look very bare. They face forward so the rider can crouch over them, hands at the front and forearms facing forward with elbows together. This is the best position for streamlined pedaling.

No gears

The moving parts of gear changers would add friction, weight, and wear to the cycle. The sizes of the two gear wheels, or cogs, front and back, are chosen by the rider at the start to fit his or her own cycling style, the track, the length of the race, the competition, and the conditions.

No brakes

There is rarely any need to brake on the special oval, banked cycle track. Brakes merely add more weight and air resistance and get in the way. The pedals can be used to slow the bike down by their fixed drive to the rear wheel.

No left fork

On a normal cycle, there are two tubes on either side of the front wheel in a Y shape, or fork. The sprint or speed cycle has only one, to cut air resistance. Like other forward-facing parts, it has a sharp leading edge and smooth sides for streamlining.

Not many spokes

The front wheel has three thin spokes. It does not have to be as strong as the rear wheel, which must transmit the turning force from the rear gear cog to the ground, so it can have less construction material.

HIGH GEARS

As you cycle along a level road on an ordinary bike, you push the pedals around once and the back wheel turns around about two times. But sprint and speed cycles have very high gear ratios or combinations. On a racing bike, one turn of the pedals turns the back wheel around four, five, or even more times!

SUPERBIKE

Windshield
The wind is very strong at more than 120mph (200kph). The windshield pushes the rushing air up and over the driver, who is also crouched down with head forward into the wind for streamlining.

Front suspension
The front forks are tubes with springs and hydraulic (oil-filled) or pneumatic (air-filled) dampers inside, to smooth out bumps in the road.

Brake calipers
The brake lever works the calipers, which press the brake pads onto the brake disc with a squeezing, scissorlike action.

Brake discs
The brake blocks, or pads, in the calipers press onto a large metal disc that is fixed to the road wheel and turns with it, to slow it down. The friction makes the disc hot so, it has holes in it for better cooling. Most superbikes have twin discs on the front wheel.

Few spokes
Many modern motorcycles do not have bicycle-type spokes in the wheels. The whole wheel is cast from one piece of metal alloy to make it strong but light. The lighter the wheel, the faster the engine can get it turning.

Slicks
Racetracks and fast roads are usually smooth and free of mud and dirt. So the superbike's tires, or slicks, do not need tread. They are just plain, soft, sticky rubber to grip the pavement.

Wraparound
The tire surface wraps around both sides. This allows the rider to lean over at an amazing angle to balance while going around corners at great speed, with the tire still gripping the road.

In-line twin V
This engine has two cylinders, one behind the other.

Fairings
A curved plastic or metal cover wraps around the main body of the motorcycle to cut down wind resistance.

POWER, WEIGHT, AND SPEED

The key to a fast vehicle is its power-to-weight ratio. This compares the weight of the vehicle with the amount of power that its engine produces to drive it along.

A superbike might weigh about 77lbs (170kg) and have an engine that produces 160 horsepower. A family car weighs up to 10 times as much and has an engine that is half as powerful. So its power-to-weight ratio is 20 times less! No wonder superbikes are among the fastest of all vehicles.

Low handlebars
The rider crouches low over the handlebars to minimize wind resistance.

Rider's seat
This is scooped out so that the driver sits as low as possible, hunched over the fuel tank for the least wind resistance.

Exhaust
Exhaust gases and fumes from each cylinder flow along pipes that come together into one pipe, and then pass through the silencer box before emerging into the air at the back, away from the rider and passenger.

Rear suspension
The rear wheel is at the end of a long leverlike arm called a swinging, or trailing, arm. This pivots with the main chassis just behind the engine. Large springs and hydraulic dampers smooth out bumps and vibrations.

Chain drive
Toothed cogs (sprockets, or gear wheels,) and a link chain, transfer turning power from the engine between the wheels to the rear wheel. Some bikes have a spinning driveshaft instead of a chain.

Gear pedal
The rider changes gear with a foot pedal by flicking it up and down. The foot pedal on the other side applies the rear brake.

HOW MANY CCS?

A cc is a measure of volume. One cc is one cubic centimeter, that is, a cube roughly the size of a lump of sugar. Motorcycles, cars, and other vehicles have engines measured in ccs or liters (one liter is 1,000 ccs). The volume that's measured is the amount of air pushed aside as the pistons move the full distance inside their cylinders.

- A small moped or track motorcycle is 50 ccs.
- A small racing motorcycle is up to 250 ccs.
- A medium motorcycle is 500 ccs.
- A large motorcycle is 750 or 900 ccs.
- There are also superbikes of 1,000 ccs (one liter) and more!
- A small family car might have an engine size of 900–1,000 ccs (up to one liter).
- Big luxury cars are 2.5 liters or more.

F1 RACECAR

Front wing
Specially-shaped to produce a force that presses the car down onto the track.

Radio antenna
The driver and his racing team can keep in contact by radio.

Tire
F1 tires are wide and have hardly any tread. Tires for use in the wet have more tread. During a race, the tires can heat up to 230°F (110°C).

Wheel
Each wheel is held in place by a single screw-on wheelnut, which can be removed very quickly. This is so that the wheels and tires can be changed rapidly during a race.

Steering wheel
The small steering wheel is fitted with buttons and switches that enable the driver to change gear and do many other things without having to let go of the wheel.

Cockpit
The driver's cockpit is very cramped, with almost no room to move. It is so small that the driver must remove the steering wheel before he gets in or out.

Sponsor's name
Running an F1 racing team is incredibly expensive. Most of the money comes from sponsors, who pay the team to advertise their names on the cars.

Fuel tanks
The tanks on either side of the driver have a honeycomblike mesh inside. This keeps the fuel from splashing around too fast inside, which would upset the car's delicate balance.

Driver's survival cell
The driver lies in a tube-shaped survival cell or "cocoon" made of extremely strong but light composite material, with only the head and arms exposed. The cell resists breaking in a crash to protect the driver.

THE CHAMPIONSHIP MACHINE

The Formula 1 racecar can accelerate from 0–100mph (0–160kph) and brake back to a standstill, all in less than six seconds. For this, the driver only needs the first and second gears out of the six usually fitted. The fastest speeds are over 200mph (320kph). A Formula 1 race is usually about 200mi (300km) and takes up to two hours. Every aspect of the car, including steering angle and fuel tank size, is reset for each racetrack. Dozens of sensors inside the car radio send information on every aspect of its performance back to the team in the pits. This information transfer is known as telemetry. The team can then advise the driver on the return radio link.

CARS WITH WINGS

Just as the wings of a plane lift it upward into the air, the wings on an F1 car push it down onto the track. This is because of their shape. On a plane, the top of the wing is curved and the underside is flat, which means that the air presses less on the top than on the bottom, so the wing is pushed upward. F1 car wings are mounted the other way up, so that the force pushes them downward. This helps the car to grip without slowing it down too much, and gives the driver more control when cornering. The wings and the body shape produce so much force that at 150mph (240kph) the car could race upside-down on a ceiling without falling off!

Engine
F1 engines are incredibly powerful, but they must also be as light as possible to help the car go faster.

Wing angle
The size and angle of each wing is altered to fit the type of circuit, depending on whether it has mostly long, fast straights, or slow, twisting bends.

Back wing
Like the wing at the front, this helps to keep the car on the track.

Exhaust manifold
The exhaust gases flow out of the engine to the tailpipe.

Brake
As well as traveling fast, the car must be able to slow down quickly. When the driver presses the brake pedal, special pads press onto large metal discs to slow down the wheels.

TRACK STARS

Many different types of cars race around circuits. As well as Formula One (F1), there are also Formula Two, Formula Three, and smaller formulas. Rally and touring cars (right) might look more like normal family cars—but they go much, much faster!

9

STRETCH LIMOUSINE

SUPER-LIMO

Some limousines are even longer than the one shown here. The record is the Ohrberg super-limo at 100ft (30m)—the same length as a blue whale! It has 26 wheels, a king-sized water bed, and a swimming pool! But it's too long to drive on most ordinary roads. It is mainly used for exhibitions and publicity events.

Intercom
Passengers can see and talk to the driver—but the driver cannot necessarily see the passengers!

Engine
A big, heavy car needs a strong, powerful engine, about 3–5 liters—that's twice as big as a family saloon. It usually takes gasoline instead of diesel for quieter, smoother running.

Soft ride
The suspension is specially softened and dampened so that the ride in the limo is as smooth and comfortable as possible.

Safety button
The driver or passenger can close and lock all windows and doors using just one button. This stops excited fans or curious sightseers from getting into the car.

S.O.S.
A red alert button informs police on a special emergency radio channel in case there is a robbery or kidnap attempt on the rich or famous passengers.

THE STRETCHED PART

Originally the "stretch" limousine was made by taking an existing luxury car, cutting it in half and welding extra panels into the gaps to make it longer. Then a new top-class interior was fitted with leather seats, luxurious carpets, and all the trimmings. Today, various specialized vehicle-makers build limos exactly to the owner's specifications. Some have fold-out beds so that they can become a luxury hotel on wheels!

Office on the move
On long trips, the limo can be a place to work. It can be fitted with a computer linked to the Internet, and a VCR so that movie or music star passengers can watch their latest movies or videos.

Radio links
Various antennae send and receive signals for radio, TV, telephone, Internet, and also private encrypted (secrecy-coded) radio and walkie-talkie channels.

Tinted windows
The windows of the passenger compartment are tinted and have a reflective coating. People trying to see in from the outside can only see their own faces. The windows are often bulletproof, too.

Comforts of home
The limo has a carphone, a TV (with satellite, of course), a sound system, a bar, hot drinks, and many other comforts.

Expert driver
The driver, or chauffeur, must be specially-trained not only to drive safely and within the law, but also to start and stop very smoothly and to guide the long limo around awkward turns and avoid sharp corners.

Keeping cool and quiet
Air-conditioning and heating keeps passengers cool when it is hot and warm in cold weather. It also filters out the smoke and fumes from traffic jams. Special body panels and thick windows keep out the noise.

WHO BUYS A STRETCH LIMO?

Whoever wants one and has enough money! However, it is a very expensive "toy" to leave sitting in the garage. And it may not get through the barrier at the local supermarket car park. This is why 9 out of 10 large limousines are owned by vehicle rental companies. A limo can be rented by the hour, day, week, or longer. The driver costs extra, too. Big limos are hired for film and music stars, bosses of big companies, royalty, presidents, politicians, and public figures—and ordinary people who decide to splash out on a special day—like a wedding.

4X4 -FOUR- WHEEL DRIVE

Silencer
This box in the exhaust pipe makes the waste gases and fumes from the engine slower and quieter. It may also contain a CAT (catalytic convertor) with special substances that remove some of the most dangerous chemicals in the fumes.

ATTs
All terrain tires have thicker, chunkier tread than normal road tires. They give good all-purpose grip on a variety of surfaces, from highways to plowed fields.

Chassis
Steel box girders make the car's chassis, or framework, very strong and rigid, so that it can take knocks from rocks and potholes.

Rear door
Some rear doors are hinged to the roof so they lift up in one piece. Others are horizontal two-part so the window section folds up and the lower part hinges down to form a tailgate platform. Others are vertical two-part, hinged at each side so they open in the middle.

Rear drive
The rear drive, or half shafts, turn the rear road wheels when the vehicle is in RWD or 4WD mode.

Light cages
If a 4x4 is used off-road it may skid and bump into trees, posts, and other objects. Wire cages around the lights prevent their coverings and bulbs from being smashed. It's easier to straighten out the wire cage than to replace the bulb and cover.

Limited slip diff
This box of gear cogs stops the vehicle from getting bogged down in slippery mud.

Suspension
4x4s have strong, stiff suspension to cope with bumps and holes on rough ground and also with the heavy loads they may carry.

Prop shaft
The propeller shaft carries the turning force from the engine back to the rear road wheels.

WHY 4WD?

A normal family car is 2WD or two-wheel drive—only two of the road wheels are turned by the engine. In small cars, it may be the front two (FWD), in larger ones it's the rear two (RWD). In a 4WD (four-wheel drive) vehicle all four road wheels are made to turn by the engine. This allows much more power to get through to the road, giving improved grip or traction. The vehicle has a better grip on slippery mud and ice, and more control in going up and down very steep hills and getting out of potholes or over rocks and roots. It also allows heavier loads to be carried.

However, 4WD uses up much more fuel. This is because the engine has to turn and work an extra set of road wheel drive parts. So most 4WDs have a lever or button that switches to 2WD for smooth roads, to save fuel—and wear and tear.

Head restraint
As a 4x4 travels over rough ground, the passengers bump and move around. Shaped restraints help to steady their heads so that they can avoid neck pain and whiplash injuries.

Engine
Most 4x4s have diesel engines. They may be heavier and noisier than gasoline engines, but they are usually more reliable and also need less servicing and maintenance.

Drive control
The driver uses a stickshift to change between FWD, RWD, and 4WD.

Front drive
The front drive shafts turn the front road wheels when the vehicle is in FWD or 4WD mode.

Disc brakes
A big, heavy car like a 4x4 needs strong brakes, so it is equipped with disc brakes all around. These are power-assisted, which means that the driver's pressure on the foot pedal is boosted by hydraulic pressure supplied by the engine.

Even more Grip

Four wheels turning may not be enough in very slippery conditions like ice and snow. So special snow chains are wrapped around the tires to give even more grip.

LIMITED SLIP DIFF

In a 2WD vehicle, the wheels on either side of the axle can rotate at different speeds while still being driven by the engine. This is called the diff or differential. It can cause trouble when off-road. Imagine the left back wheel of the car is in a very slippery place, such as on ice. It has hardly anything to grip, so it can spin almost freely. The diff allows it to do this, while the right back wheel—which is on dry pavement and can grip—simply keeps still. The vehicle is stuck! This doesn't happen when a vehicle has limited or non-slip diff. Only a limited difference is allowed between the speeds of the two wheels. Beyond this the drive is still applied to the slower wheel, which hauls the vehicle out of the rut, so it's no longer stuck.

FRONT-LOADER

Lights
To get the job done on time, the front-loader and driver may have to work nights. The lights move with the bucket so it is always brightly lit. There are also lights at the rear, and the driver's seat swivels around, too, because a front-loader spends plenty of time in reverse.

Hydraulic hoses
High-pressure oil is pumped along these flexible pipes into the cylinders to work the rams. The pipes bend so that the front-loader booms and bucket can move. They have steel mesh inside their walls for extra strength.

Bucket tilt rams
The bucket tilts up or down when these hydraulic rods and pistons push or pull on it.

"Artic"
The front-loader is articulated—it has a hinge or joint in the middle. It steers not by twisting the wheels, but by moving the whole front end, including the bucket, to one side or the other.

Bucket
An average bucket is 7 or 8ft (2.5–3m) wide. It is not always full of earth or rocks. The front-loader can be used to carry loads, such as bags of cement or blocks of bricks, around the site.

SWL
Most construction machines have SWLs, safe working loads. A front-loader may have a SWL of 7–8 tons for a bucket.

Main booms
These link the front-loader body to the bucket. They are moved by hydraulic rams.

Raise-lower rams
This pair of hydraulic rods and pistons pushes the booms and raises the bucket more than 8ft (3m) into the air, so it can tip its contents into a dump truck or earthmover.

BUCKETS OF BUCKETS
The bucket shown here is a typical all-purpose design for gouging into and lifting soil, earth, small rocks, gravel, and sand. There are many other bucket designs for different jobs. A smoothing bucket is lower and wider to scrape a large area level. A basket bucket is made of steel bars like a cage for lifting lighter, looser material such as hay, straw, and household refuse.

Cab
The driver sits in an air-conditioned, vibration-proofed, and sound-proofed cab. This protects the driver from being deafened and shaken up by a day's work.

Controls
Hand levers or buttons control the bucket's movements. Floor pedals and the steering wheel make the whole front-loader move around.

Engine
A heavy-duty diesel engine provides the power for turning the wheels, and for the hydraulic system to raise and lower the bucket. The engine produces about 180–200 horsepower (almost three times the power of a small family car).

Huge tires
A big front-loader has tires taller than the average adult. They have deep tread to grip soft ground. Sometimes they are filled partly with water for extra weight and grip.

FRONT-LOADERS GALORE
Front-loaders, excavators, and other load-movers find jobs in all kinds of work, from piling up scrapped cars, to scooping up gravel and sand for building, to scraping up sea salt from shallow coastal lagoons.

IT'S ALL DONE BY HYDRAULICS
Many large vehicles and machines rely on hydraulic systems. They use oil under very high pressure. It is pumped along a pipe or hose into a large metal tube-shaped cylinder. Closely fitting inside the cylinder is a rod-shaped piston. As the oil is forced into the cylinder it pushes the piston in front of it. The piston usually has a long metal rod attached to it, and the other end is linked to the part that moves. The pressure is so great that if a hose sprang a leak, the thin jet of oil spurting out of it would blast a small hole straight through the body of a person standing in the way.

Like our own muscles, hydraulic pistons can only push. For two-way movement there are two pistons that rock the part to be moved like a seesaw. Or two pistons face each other in the same long cylinder, and the oil is pumped from one end of the cylinder to the other. This gives push-pull power.

EIGHTEEN-WHEELER

Air horns
Compressed air blasts out of the horns to make a sound heard more than 1mi (2km) away.

Cockpit
There are lots of dials and controls. The dashboard looks more like a plane cockpit or flight deck.

CB radio
Drivers keep in touch with each other by CB, or citizen's band radio. They talk and pass the time, discuss the weather and road conditions, or their trucks and loads, and warn each other of traffic jams or accidents.

Gears
There may be 10, 12, or more gears to help the truck pull away uphill with its 40-ton load, or cruise down the highway at its maximum speed.

Driver's seat
The driver's seat is reinforced and strengthened with a pilotlike safety harness for a seat belt to cope with the amazing acceleration and cornering speed.

Limiter
Working trucks are fitted with speed limiters since in many countries they are not allowed to go as fast as ordinary cars.

Engine
The giant turbo-charged diesel engine may be 10 times the size of a family car engine. Some speed trucks are even fitted with jet engines like those used on fighter aircraft!

Square shape
This truck has few curves. Its design is flat-sided and squared-off. This makes it look strong and powerful. But it is not so good for speed and fuel economy.

Shiny chrome
On a show truck like this one, many of the parts are coated with chrome metal for a shiny, hard-wearing appearance. But that means a lot of polish to keep the vehicle looking clean!

TRUCK SHAPES

In the days before power-assisted controls, truck driving was a job for big, strong people—usually men. The trucks were designed to look masculine, powerful, and even menacing, with boxlike shapes. However, these designs are very bad at pushing aside air smoothly. For every half a mile a big, boxy truck travels, it must push aside about 20 tons of air. This high amount of resistance uses up huge amounts of fuel. Modern trucks have more curved, streamlined shapes to save fuel.

Exhaust stack
Exhaust fumes are dangerous—deadly if breathed in—because they contain poisonous gases such as carbon monoxide. They must be vented from an opening higher than all occupied parts of the vehicle. So this exhaust stack is about 11ft (4m) high!

Sleeper
This eighteen-wheeler has a small room just behind the driver's cab. It has beds cabinets, a sink, and a small stove. On long trips, the driver and co-driver can rest here or pull into an overnight truck stop.

Days on the Road
Truck drivers may spend days driving their rig from coast to coast, so small personal comforts are very important.

Wheels
The enormous wheels and tires are chest-high to an adult. Some trucks have two pairs of front wheels, one behind the other—and both pairs turn with the steering wheel.

Artic link
The truck is designed to haul a trailer equipped with an articulated link, sometimes called the "fifth wheel." The front of the trailer hooks into and rests on a large metal disc at the rear of the truck itself, which is known as the tractor unit. This allows the whole vehicle to bend at the artic link.

Fuel tank
The fuel tank is made of shiny chrome (on a working truck it would be dull gray or black). It holds more than 140gal (2,000l) of diesel fuel, which is 40 times as much as an ordinary car.

Electrics and hydraulics
The rear of the truck has connectors and sockets for the wires and hydraulic hoses on the trailer unit. These allow the driver to control the lights, brakes, and other equipment on the trailer.

POWERED EVERYTHING

A large vehicle like this truck is so big and heavy that the steering, brakes, and other features are powered or power-assisted. For example, the driver puts on the brakes by pressing the brake pedal. But the driver's leg and foot do not produce all the physical force necessary to press the brake pads onto the brake discs. Pushing the brake pedal activates switches called actuators that are connected to the hydraulic system driven by the engine. The hydraulic system's oil-filled cylinders and hoses produce the huge force needed to press the brake pads onto the discs.

MOUNTAIN RAILWAY

Pantograph contact
The sliding bar contact picks up electricity from the current wire. The folding arm keeps the bar in good contact with the current wire to keep the electricity flowing and reduce sparks.

Suspension cable and current wire
A strong suspension cable holds up a current wire designed to carry the electric current.

Insulator
Ceramic insulators keep electricity from leaking down the pylon into the ground. They are shaped like stacked cones so that water and ice do not build up on them, causing a short circuit.

Passenger door
Passengers enter and leave by many doors along the side of the car. This makes station stops quicker.

Snow shovels
Angled blades push loose snow off the rails and out of the way as the car moves along.

HIGHER AND CHEAPER

Mountain railways are difficult to build and maintain. The track must be fairly straight and may have to be blasted out of the steep rock. It is a constant battle to keep snow and ice off the track and the overhead power wires often ice up, too. A cheaper alternative for some regions, especially tourist resorts and winter sports centers, is the cable car. This is not affected by snow and ice on the ground. It can't work in very windy or stormy weather, but few vacationers are out in this type of weather.

De-icer
Chemical sprays remove ice from the track and rack so the car can keep moving even in very cold conditions.

Motor
The electric motor runs on current picked up from the overhead wire. Sets or trains of gears connect it to the rack drive cog and the main wheels of the car. The motor can help braking by altering the way electricity flows through it so that they resist being turned instead of causing a turning motion. This is known as rheostatic braking, and adds to the general braking system so the car does not race away downhill.

Air horns
Very loud horns blow to scare animals off the track or to alert people to the train's approach.

OVER THE SNOW
In one type of cable car, the cars are attached to the cable, which moves around in an endless loop carrying all the cars with it. In another, each car has a motor and its wheels move along the stationary cable.

Two cabs
When the train reaches the stop or station at the top of the line, the driver goes to the other end of the car and gets in the cab there to drive it back down again.

Toothed rack
A strip or rack of teeth runs along the middle of the track between the rails. These are gripped by the rack drive cog on the underside of the train for non-slip propulsion.

Inclined track
The track slants at the same angle all the way up the line. Otherwise the drive cog would not grip the track.

28

Wheel cog
This gear wheel is rotated by the motor and then makes the wheel spin around. It can also be used as part of the braking system.

Rack drive cog
The teeth of this gear wheel fit between the teeth of the track rack to haul the car up the slope.

TGV

Suspension (catenary) cable
This cable holds and supports the current wire below it. The suspension cable is made of metals designed to withstand the strain of hanging and being blown around by the wind. The current wire is weaker, but made of metals able to carry, or conduct, electricity well.

Current (power) wire
This carries the very high voltages of electric current picked up by the train as it passes below. The current strength may be 25,000 volts or more—2,000 times the strength of normal household mains electricity.

Pylon
Tall towers made of steel or concrete beams hold up the electric power lines.

Driver's cab
The driver's display monitors the conditions in the electrical circuits, motors, and other equipment. It also monitors the brakes, automatic doors, and other machinery farther back in the passenger cars.

Drive gear train
Gear wheels slow down the spinning motion of the traction motors and make it more powerful to turn the drive wheels of the power car.

Wheels
Railway wheels have flanges on the inside that project down onto the inner side of the rail so the wheel does not slip off.

STRAIGHT AHEAD
High-speed trains must have even straighter tracks than normal trains—with very gradual curves—or they would tip over as they went around corners.

FASTER TRAINS
Modern electric passenger trains whiz through city and countryside at tremendous speed. The French TGV (*train à grande vitesse* or "very fast train") has reached 320mph (515kph) on a special speed run. Other high-speed services that reach 190mph (300kph) include the Eurostar between Britain and Continental Europe through the Channel Tunnel, ICE in Germany, and the Bullet trains in Japan.

DC pantograph
In some countries, the current wire carries DC or direct current. This flows in one direction. It is picked up by the pantograph.

Compressor
This produces high-pressure air to work the brakes.

AC pantograph
This pantograph picks up the AC, alternating current. This means the direction of the electricity switches back and forth many times each second, usually 50 or 60.

Inter-car bogie
Most train cars have two-wheeled bogies, one at each end. This train has a bogie under the join between one car and the next. This method means fewer wheels and parts, and less weight.

Wheel bogie
Railway wheels are usually in sets of four, two pairs, on a chassis called a bogie. This is hinged so it can turn to the side as the train goes around a curve. It also has springs to absorb vibrations and bumps from the rails so that the passengers have a smooth ride.

Rectifiers
These electrical devices change AC into DC to work the lights, controls, hydraulics, brakes, and other systems.

Transformers
Very high voltage AC is transformed or stepped down to lower voltages for the traction motors and other equipment.

Traction motors
These extremely powerful electric motors drive the wheels through a chain of gears.

Passenger car
Passengers sit in comfortable airline-type seats in a car that is soundproofed and air-conditioned.

LOCOMOTIVES

A train is made up of a locomotive, also known as a power car or traction unit, pulling passenger cars, goods (cargo) wagons, and other units behind it. The locomotive is powered in various ways—

- By steam power.

- A diesel locomotive or unit has a diesel engine that drives the wheels through a gearbox. It can be heard changing gear like a car.

- A diesel-electric locomotive has a diesel engine that drives an alternator or generator to make electricity, which is fed to electric motors that turn the wheels. Electric motors work well at all speeds, so a gearbox is not needed.

- An electric locomotive uses only electric motors, as in the train shown here.

JETSKI

Handlebars
The rider grips these and steers the craft with them like on a motorcycle. As the handlebars turn to one side, they swivel the jet nozzle so it points to that side, making the craft veer around.

Twistgrip throttle
The handlebar grip is twisted to open the engine throttle and make the jetski go faster. But there are no brakes!

Spray rail
This curved shelflike part reduces the spray.

Fuel filler cover
Gasoline is poured into the fuel tank through the fuel inlet under this cover.

Battery
The battery provides electricity to start the engine, like in a car or electric-start motorcycle, and also for any lights it has.

Engine
Most jetskis have modified motorcycle or similar engines, with the gearing changed to fit the revolving speed of the impeller.

Exhaust
The exhaust gases are piped from the engine along the side of the jetski and out at the back—safely away from rider and passenger.

Driveshaft
The turning motion of the engine spins the drive- or prop- (propeller) shaft, which turns the impeller at its rear end.

TRICKS AND STUNTS

The jetski is perfect for all kinds of tricky riding and exciting stunts. Experts can make the craft leap out of the water and spin around in mid-air, or ride up a waterski ramp and do a somersault. Races are held around buoys, often with a line of buoys close together where the rider has to slalom between them. In the group of maneuvers called "submarines," the rider makes the craft tilt nose-up, bounce into the air, and then dive nose-down under the surface, still holding on. He or she can even turn around while underwater and pop up again some distance away.

Rider's seat
The rider sits or kneels astride the front seat, crouched over the handlebars and with knees and feet down in the foot wells on either side. He or she leans to the side to help steer the jetski.

Passenger's seat
A passenger can kneel or sit behind the rider. Like on a motorcycle, the passenger usually stays still and upright, and lets the rider lean and balance the craft.

Passenger grab handle
The passenger holds onto these handles on either side.

Side rail
This type of jetski has sides with side rails along the top, for protection and streamlining. Other types have open sides like a motorcycle.

Tow hitch
The craft can tow a small boat or a water-skier.

Impeller
This is a long, strong fan (similar to a propeller) that works as a high-speed water pump. It spins to suck in, or impel, water into its pipe or tube through a wide opening on the underside of the craft. It then forces the water out toward the rear through the nozzle as a fast, powerful, narrow jet.

Jet nozzle
Water from the impeller blasts out of the jet nozzle with great force and speed, pushing the craft along. The nozzle swings from side to side for steering, controlled by the handlebars.

Foot well
The rider and passenger put their legs on either side of the seat, and their knees and feet in the wells along each side.

A NEW TYPE OF WATER CRAFT

Jetskis are like water skis with motorcycle handles and seats, powered by a water jet. They are also known as waterbikes or PWC, personal water craft. They were developed in the late 1960s by American motorcycle racer Clay Jacobson and the Japanese Kawasaki motorcycle company. Their idea was to combine a motorcycle, snowmobile, and water skis into a one-person water vehicle that was fun to ride and race, and didn't cause injuries if the rider fell off. The first craft went on sale in 1973.

23

OFFSHORE POWERBOAT

Cockpit
The driver and co-driver sit in the cockpit with lots of dials, switches, buttons, and screens in front of them. They rely on these instruments because the waves and spray mean it can be difficult to see.

Strengthened hull
The offshore powerboat is a brutal machine. It smashes through the ocean waves at speeds of over 90mph (150kph). The main body, or hull, must be light yet extremely strong to withstand the battering, since waves at this speed are like sledgehammer blows. It is usually made of aluminum or carbon fiber.

Spray rail
This rail along the hull pushes most of the spray and water aside so it does not break over the boat itself.

THE RACE
Powerboat races may be around a marked-out course or across the open sea from one town or island to another. This type of racing looks glamorous, but it is very tiring and stressful.

SAFETY FIRST
Speeding powerboats don't lie in the water and push it aside. They plane, or skim, over the surface. Only the very rear parts with the screws and rudders dip into the water. However, the boat can't avoid big waves, and these produce huge shocks as the boat plows through them. For this reason, the crew must tough and in good shape. The driver steers the powerboat, using satellite navigation and many other electronic aids. The co-driver controls the speed of the engines using their throttles and adjusts the boat's trim. The crew are attached to a "kill switch" by long cords. If they are accidentally thrown out of their seats, the kill switch stops the engine so that the powerboat does not race away out of control across the sea.

F1 BOATS

Offshore powerboats have incredible strength and power for racing across the open sea. And just as Formula 1 is the top level for racing cars around a special track, Formula 1 powerboats are the top level on water. They race in sheltered waters around marker buoys, following a course similar to a Formula 1 car circuit, for 50–60 laps. They are small and streamlined with catamarans—two long, slim hulls side by side under the main body. F1 boats have outboard engines, attached by a hinged bracket at the back. They can reach speeds of more than 150mph (250kph.)

Airfoil wing
The roof of the cockpit is an airfoil wing. It helps to lift the boat's hull farther out of the water for greater speed.

Ram air intake
Air for the engines is scooped in by the intakes, which are positioned away from the main spray areas.

Engine access covers
The covers lift off to reveal the engines for adjusting, maintenance, repair, and installing new engines.

Tailgate rams
The rear, or tailgate, of the powerboat is hinged to the main hull. As the boat changes speed or alters its direction to the wind, the front of the hull lifts up and planes by varying amounts. The angle of the tailgate is automatically adjusted by hydraulic rams to keep the screws in their best position in the water.

Rudders
Twin rudders are positioned just behind the screws. This is the best position for making the boat turn sharply as it steers around a buoy or small island during a race.

Gearbox
The turning speed of the engine is changed by gears into the best turning speed for the screw (propeller).

Screws
Twin screws thrust the boat forward.

Trim flaps
Wind, waves, and currents can make the boat slew, or move diagonally, even when the steering wheel is set straight ahead. So it is "trimmed" with small rudderlike flaps, or tabs, to counteract these forces and make it travel straight ahead with the wheel in the central position.

CRUISE LINER

Restaurant
Many cruise liners serve excellent food and drinks. In addition to the main restaurant, there are also fast-food outlets, snack bars, and cafes. You can get a meal or drink any time of day or night.

Bulkhead
A bulkhead is a wall or partition across a boat or ship from side to side. In case of an accident, the doors and other openings in it can be closed to make the ship watertight.

Patio deck
Deck chairs and tables near the restaurant and bar area are for eating, drinking, visiting, and enjoying the view.

Pool deck
There's no shortage of water—the swimming pool is topped up from the sea. Of course, the water is filtered and treated with germ-killing chemicals first!

Sun deck
As the liner speeds along, the front end, or bow, is very windy, but the rear deck is usually sheltered. Passengers can laze here out of the breeze.

Rudder
This moveable flap steers the ship. If it swings to the left the water pushes against it and makes the rear of the liner move to the right, swinging the whole liner to the left.

Screw
As the screw, or propeller, turns, it forces water backward past its angled blades and so pushes the ship forward.

Engine room
The huge diesel or gas turbine engines are deep in the rear of the liner. Their noise and vibrations are insulated from the rest of the ship. The heat from the exhaust gases is used for the ship's heating system before the gases are sent through the funnel to the open air.

THE "BIG SHOP"

A cruise liner for about 2,000 passengers may have almost 1,000 crew to look after them and the ship. That's 3,000 people to feed and supply with drinks. The ship must take plenty of supplies in case the engines fail and it's late back to port. An average shopping list for a two-week voyage might include—

- 12 tons of potatoes, pasta, and rice
- 25 tons of vegetables
- 40 tons of fresh fruit
- 25 tons of meat and fish
- 30,000 bottles of wine
- 60,000 pints of beer

Radome
Radar, radio, and satellite navigation equipment are protected inside a dome against wind, rain, and other severe weather. The radio signals pass easily through the dome.

Bridge
The captain and crew have a good all-round view from the bridge, high up near the front of the ship.

Lifeboats
By law, the lifeboats, liferafts, and similar emergency equipment should have a seat or place for every person onboard the ship. The crew give regular demonstrations of what do to in an accident.

Premier cabins
The luxury or executive cabins are larger and more comfortable than the economy cabins. They are higher in the ship so there are fewer stairs to climb to the public areas and they have better views from the portholes.

Indoor pool
The pool is part of the fitness suite which also has workout and gym equipment, a massage table, sunbeds, and a sauna.

Cinema-theatre
Movies, videos, songs, shows, speeches, band performances, discos, and other events take place in the theater. This provides entertainment in the evenings or when the weather is bad.

Economy cabins
Smaller cabins lower in the liner have less of a view from the porthole (window). If they are interior cabins they have no view at all! This is why they cost less than the premier cabins.

THE FALL AND RISE OF THE CRUISE LINER

During the early 1900s, when few people traveled by air, the cruise liner was very popular. It was a floating hotel that took vacationers to faraway places, which they visited from the liner by boarding smaller boats.

With the rise of jetliners, all-inclusive vacations, and car rental in the late 1900s, people became more adventurous travelers. Cruise ships seemed slow and restricted. You had to go where the captain took you, and for days at a time you were stuck onboard with only a limited amount to see and do.

However, we are now experiencing a revival in luxury cruising, with some of the biggest and best-equipped new ships ever. They are more like floating cities than floating hotels. Now more than 10 million people enjoy pleasure cruises every year.

HYDROFOIL

HYDROFOIL FERRIES

Around the world, hydrofoil ferries take passengers on short, fast trips. The larger ones carry 300 passengers at speeds of more than 40 mph (60 kph). Jet hydrofoils, or jetfoils, have water jets, or turbines, instead of screws. Hydrofoils are especially useful for carrying people between the mainland and nearby islands.

Wheel house
This is where the controls are. They are a combination of those from a ship, an airplane, and a car.

The helm
As in a normal boat, the wheel, or helm, makes the rudder at the rear of the craft swing from side to side for steering at low speed. It also twists the front hydrofoil and its struts from side to side for steering at high speed.

Bow mooring cleats
Ropes, or lines, from the shore are tied around these cleats when the hydrofoil comes alongside its mooring place, or berth.

Hull
The hull sits in the water at low speed, but rises above it into the air on the hydrofoil struts as the craft picks up speed.

BOAT ON SKIS

The hydrofoil is an underwater wing. It works in the same way as an airplane wing or airfoil. Its shape is curved from front to back on top, and flatter from front to back on the underside. As the foil moves forward, water must flow farther over the longer curved upper surface than underneath. So water moves faster above the foil than below. This faster flow creates less pressure above the foil, with the result that the foil is sucked upward by a force called lift. At high speed, the lift is enough to raise the whole craft out of the water. This hugely reduces the water friction, or drag, along the hull, which slows down a normal boat. It also creates a smoother ride. But hydrofoils cannot travel in stormy conditions.

Radar

Stern mooring cleat
The craft is moored by this cleat when it arrives at its destination.

Life belts
If someone falls into the water, a lifebelt on its rope helps rescue them.

Skylights
During daylight the middle of the cabin is lit by these windows in the roof deck. They can be used as emergency exits in case of an accident.

Screw
The spinning angled blades push the water backward and drive the craft forward.

Engine
A diesel engine provides the power to turn the screw and propel the hydrofoil along. Its construction is strong and heavy since weight is less important in ships and boats than land vehicles.

Prop shaft
The shaft is spun by the engine and has the screw (propeller) at its end. On a hydrofoil, the shaft is extra-long and angled down and back so the screw stays in the water as the craft rises with speed to "cruising height."

Hydrofoil
This is the name for the skilike part underneath, and the craft was named after it. It has an airfoil shape that creates a lifting force as it moves through the water, and its depth and angle are constantly adjusted by computer.

Side board
Passengers and crew can enter through the door or walk alongside the craft and onto the shore.

HI-TECH HYDROFOILS

The type of hydrofoil shown here is called a submerged-foil. The whole of each hydrofoil stays under the water. Because the foils are not as wide as the boat, there is a risk of the craft tipping over on its side. "Pingers" along the underside of the craft beam ultrasonic clicks down onto the water surface, which reflects them back to sensors. (This system, called sound-radar, or sonar, is also used to measure the depth of the seabed.) The onboard computer constantly measures the height of the hydrofoil and its angle, or tilt, from front to back and side to side. It then adjusts the tilt of the foils so the craft stays steady and safe.

SUPERTANKER

THE GIANT IN PORT

Supertankers are so huge and awkward to maneuver that they do not come into small harbors. Large terminals are built for them where there is plenty of room and the water is deeper. Small, powerful tug boats push them into position.

Crew gangway
Crew members can quickly reach any part of the deck along the gangways. They often use bicycles, since the whole ship may be more than 800ft (300m) long.

Pipes
A maze of pipes connects the various tanks and pumps with the connectors for loading or unloading the oil.

Pumps
Various pumps force the oil into the tanks when loading at the oil production platform, then suck it out again when the supertanker reaches its destination—the oil refinery or storage depot.

Mooring winches
Thick cables, or hawsers, are used to moor the ship against its platform or terminal. They are pulled in by powerful winches and stored below deck on the voyage.

NEDLLOYD ROUEN

Anchor
The huge anchor is lowered to the seabed when the supertanker needs to stay in the same place but cannot moor, or tie up. The thrusters and main screws might also be used to keep the ship still or "on station."

Thrusters
These small propellers, or screws, in the side of the hull make the boat swing sideways to help with steering.

Valves
The oil is pumped on and off through connectors with valves inside to make it flow the correct way.

SAFETY AND POLLUTION

The supertanker may be gigantic, but it floats easily. Oil is lighter than water and floats on top of it. However, this can cause huge problems. A supertanker accident can release vast quantities of thick crude oil that floats on the sea in slicks. It kills fish, sea birds, and other marine life. If it washes ashore it can devastate coastal regions and destroy coastal wildlife. Newer tankers have hulls with double skins to keep them from leaking oil in an accident, and they also have very strict fire precautions.

Satellite and radio links
The ship is in direct contact with several types of satellites. They include telecom satellites for telephone, television, and computer links, the GPS (global positioning system) for satellite navigation, and specialist marine satellites that provide detailed weather reports or emergency channels in case of an accident.

Funnel
Exhaust gases from the engines blow up the funnel and away into the air.

Crew quarters
When they aren't on duty the crew live, rest, sleep, and eat here.

Cargo crane
A small crane helps to lift specialist equipment, food, and other supplies on and off the ship.

Bridge
This is the control center for the ship. The captain, navigator, and other senior crew have a high, clear, all-around view of the ship and its surroundings through the large windows.

Engines and screws
The engines are at the rear of the ship, separated from the oil for safety. The ship is pushed forward by one or more screws at the rear, or stern.

Oil tanks
Oil is stored in many separate tanks that take up most of the ship. If a storm caused oil to slosh around in one huge tank, it might make the ship tip over, or capsize.

GIANTS OF THE SEAS

Crude oil is used to make fuels such as gasoline, diesel, kerosene, and paraffin, as well as tars and bitumen for roads, paints and pigments, plastics, mineral rubber, and hundreds of other substances. Many oil reserves are under the seabed. Ocean drilling platforms bore holes down to harvest the crude oil. A supertanker takes it onboard and carries it to an oil terminal where there are storage tanks and refineries for treatment. Supertankers are the biggest ships on the seas. Some weigh over 300,000 tons, and are more than 800ft (300m) long. They take 2–3mi (3–5km) to steer around a corner and 3–6mi (5–10km) to stop. They are sometimes called ULCCs, ultra large crude carriers.

Index